Contents

C000000760

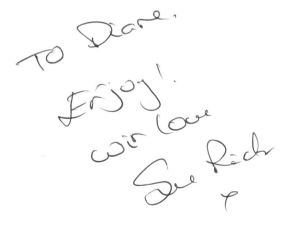

Special Thanks

I wish to thank all those who have given me endless encouragement to write. You have all been amazing and given me so much love, support, and reasons to feel very blessed.

There are so many people I would like to thank, and so if I have discussed book writing with you, or you have asked me to write; please recognise my thanks. Big thanks go to Nancy and Philippa who first nudged me to write this. There are some people who I would like to mention specifically. Firstly my two amazing sons Paul and David who have been such an example to me of how our way of thinking is the foundation of happiness. Their joy of life, success and love for people is an example to us all. Thank you to my parents John and Vivienne who have been such a huge support with everything, thank you so much. I also thank Nancy and Steve for fun times, holidays, relaxation and time to reflect! Nancy is not only my Sister but my soul sister too. Thank you for the great people that I have worked with who have been such a part of making the books that have been living in my head and are now becoming a reality. Special thanks go to Jacqui Blakemore who has worked tirelessly to make dreams a reality. Thank you to Joanne Henson, Chris Holland and Angela Otter for their fabulous reviews, admin and typing skills!

A special mention goes to Cathy Brown for our chats and explorations of the wonders of life. Also thanks to Nick Haines for keeping me going, Thanks to Jayne Thompson for reminding me she was waiting to see the books appear and Amanda Bower who gave me my first instruction book on how to write a book! Thanks Jayne and Claire for making it all happen! A big thank you for the mentoring skills of Nick Williams for showing me the way and Caroline Eddleston for her gifts to the world. Thanks also go to my lovely support crew who are always there; Jillie, Judy, Sue, Debbie, Kären and Auntie Jean.

More than anything thanks go to each and every one of you who have been part of my clinic, school or circle of friends who have proved the success of the system in this book.

Foreword - A Message from the Author

This book is written as a simple guide and I have found it to be invaluable both for family, friends, clients and myself.

This book started life whilst sitting with family and friends overlooking the gorgeous view of the Cornish coastline in Newquay. We were discussing what makes some people happy and what makes some struggle. I explained the three step programme that works for everyone and this led to the creation of this little book!

I am very aware of how our thoughts govern and affect our levels of happiness. This is a very simple plan of what to do. When I was younger I longed to know how to think more positively and would have been glad to know these three simple steps - so here they are for you now!

I hope that by reading and using this little book you will have the quick and easy tools to help you make a better life. You will soon acquire the skills and knowledge to enable you to turn any situation around to the positive. You will be able to cope much better and more comfortably with any given situation. And you will be capable of relying entirely on yourself for your own happiness, helping you to become more independent and break free from any reliance on any person or situation in your life.

There have been many books written on this subject and I hope that the simple and short format of this book will make it accessible for all who wish to find a better and happier way to live.

All you have to do is follow the three steps and gain the results!

It has worked for me and I hope it works for you too.

Sue Ricks

Chapter One - An Introduction to Happiness

A native American boy is talking with his grandfather.

Boy: *What do you think about the world situation?*

Grandfather: *I feel like two wolves are fighting in my heart. One is full of anger and hatred. The other is full of love, forgiveness and peace.*

Boy: *Which one will win the fight?*

Grandfather: *The one I feed*

Have you noticed when you are having a bad day, everything seems to go wrong? Well the same happens when you are having a good day too. What would your life be like if you could make every day a better day and be able to enjoy and be happier with your life?

What would it be like if you could get on with more people? Would you like to feel at ease? Would you like to have more confidence in yourself? Would it be nice to like yourself more?

If so, then this book is written for you.

Can Being Happy be Simple? Can Everyone do it?

Well maybe and maybe not. What if it just depended on what you have been taught to think or how you choose to think? Is there a simple plan that can change lives and get results immediately? I believe that there is.

As a teenager I really found life hard. I struggled in so many ways and I now wish I knew this simple programme as it is so easy to do.

Anyone can do it, anywhere and at any time. It is as simple as one, two, three!

I have now been recommending this to people for over five years and have witnessed how quickly the system can be introduced into everyday life. It is easy to do and you will reap the rewards in a very short time.

A client of mine was finding that she was feeling unhappy, depressed and lacking in motivation. Within two days of learning the steps she had made a significant change to her life. She reported she was feeling happier, more positive and enjoying looking forward in life. It is never too late to learn a new trick or two!

I have personally found it excellent and professionally it has helped hundreds of my clients and students. The simplicity of it belies its effectiveness.

As the saying goes "the best things come in little packages" and this little parcel of knowledge and skill can be life changing.

I suggest you read it, do it and keep doing it. It just gets better and easier with time and practice.

The book is based on the simple principle that 'like attracts like' and that when you are thinking about 'good' things, then more 'good' things tend to happen around you. However, the reverse also applies! If you are thinking about negative things - then things often keep going wrong.

Some people are deemed to be 'lucky' and others 'unlucky'. Which would you rather be?

We can make a difference to our lives by finding more appropriate things to think about. Whatever we are thinking about we are actually putting effort and energy into. In effect we 'feed' whatever we are thinking about. So the choice is ours, we can either choose to think about things that are helpful to our lives or not!

If you choose to think about things that are good for you or you decide to think about subjects that are 'safe', you will find your life becoming so much more enjoyable.

Theresa says *"I have noticed I get on so much better with people and less things bother me. I am definitely calmer."*

By following the simple steps program you will know what to do. Many people have often been told to "pull yourself together" and have been left wondering "how?" Well here's the "how"!

You can use this system for the little things in life and for bigger issues too. You are never too young or too old to learn new ways of enjoying life and making a direct influence on your own life.

Chapter Two – Three Steps to a Happier Life

Step One

Start by thinking of three things that you like about your life.

It could be anything that you enjoy, like, appreciate etc.

1)_____

2) _____

3) _____

If you are not sure what to write here – turn to the next page to see some examples.

Some Examples:

I love my family (husband, wife, partner)

I love my children

I love my parents (mother, father)

I love my house/home

I love my garden

I love my job

I love my car

I love my holidays

I love cycling

I love going to the gym

I love wildlife

I love my cat

I love my dog

I love the theatre

I love beautiful landscapes

I love art

I love my church

I love books

I love music

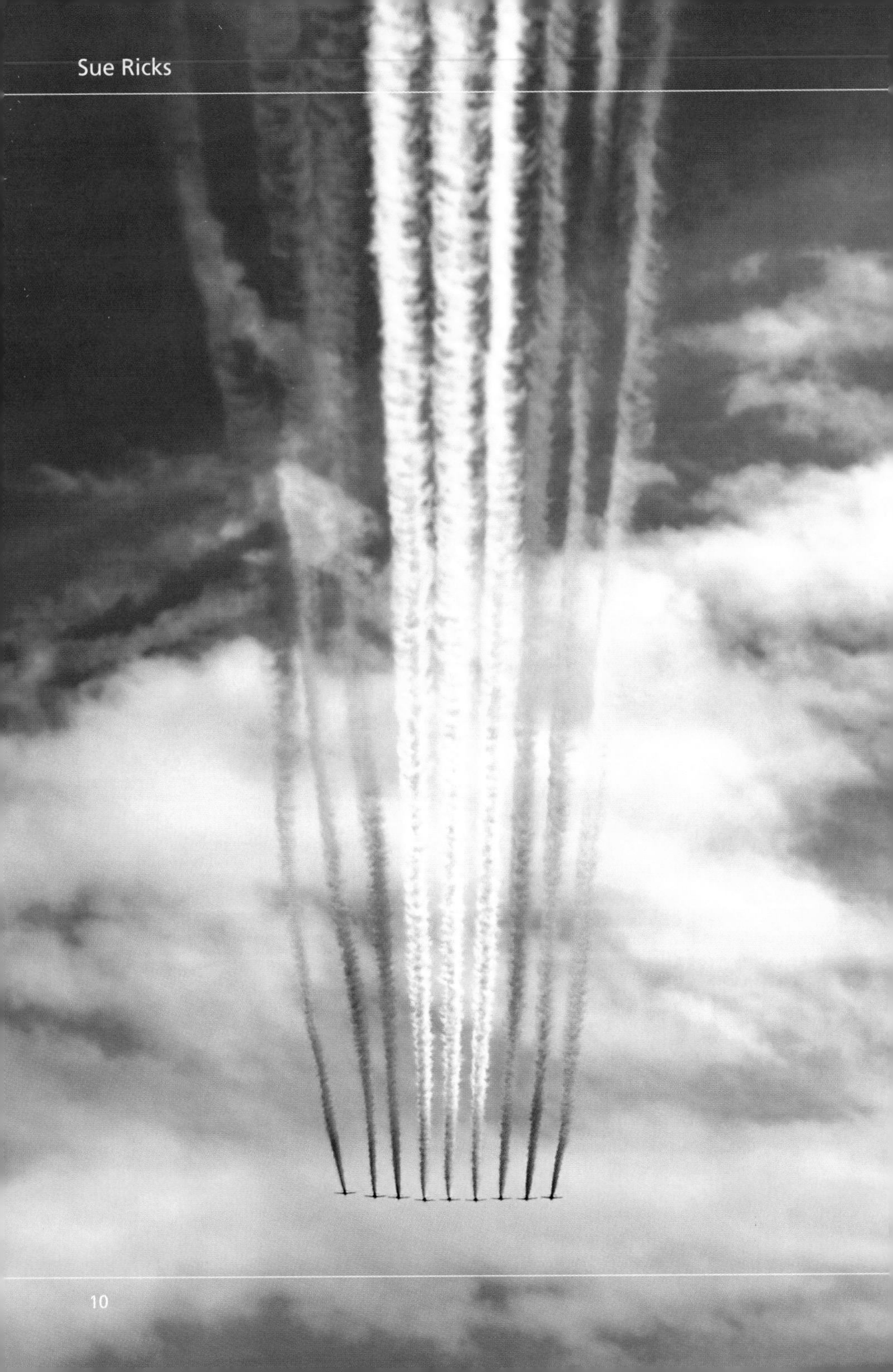

Now that you have three things that you like about your life – you are safe! You can think about these and generate more of these positive vibrations in your life. Remember 'good' attracts 'good'.

Whenever you realise that you are thinking a negative or inappropriate thought you can switch your thinking to one of these three 'safe' subjects.

If you notice you are having a negative thought:

Immediately think about your safe list of things to divert your mind to.

Exercise

List three things 'I like about my life':

1) _____

2) _____

3) _____

Repetition is a great way of being able to remember them really quickly. You will find it quicker and easier each time you recall your list.

Feel free to alter them or add new ones if you fancy a change, the more the merrier. As long as you have pre-planned your thoughts for the day, you will be prepared for any challenge.

Step Two

Now that you can safely think about three things that you like about your life, we can take this process a stage further.

The next part of the three-step programme gives you something invaluable that is often missed. So here it is for you now.

Think of something that you love or like about you!

1) _____

This could be:

> Something you like about your personality (I am kind, thoughtful, patient etc).
> A part of your body or figure you like (I love my hair, eyes, legs etc).
> Something you are good at (I love my ability to - paint, do the garden, fix computers etc).
> Something you can create/do (I make a great Sunday lunch, I am good at map reading, I am good at wrapping presents).
> Anything you like about yourself (I love my sense of humour, organising ability, generosity).

It may seem strange (or difficult) to think about something you like about yourself but this is an important factor to the three-step programme.

In our culture many of us have been brought up to put other people before ourselves. A person who thinks of, or about themselves is instantly labelled as 'selfish'. Yet it is thinking of ourselves that matters the most. If we do not think of ourselves, we can be of no real good to anyone else. We need to look after ourselves first and then others later. That way, we can be of the most benefit to other people and to ourselves.

Sue Ricks

We have also been taught that it is okay to think about the good in others. However, we may not have been encouraged to talk about or acknowledge the good in ourselves. Old phrases such as "who do you think you are" or "don't blow your own trumpet" may have previously prevented you from voicing what is great about you.

Even if you don't voice this new-found knowledge of what is great about you to anyone else, it is essential that you know in your own mind what you like about yourself. So, think of something you really like about yourself and make a note of it now.

If it takes you a while, please don't worry, however, do make sure you make the commitment to yourself to follow it through and get to know and acknowledge one thing you really like about yourself.

Once you have found something you like about yourself, repeat it several times:

I love/like _____ (about me)

Claire found this very hard at first, but as soon as she got the hang of it, it changed her life. She has previously managed to ignore her good points and had thought that everyone was better than she was. As soon as she was repeating the good thing she loved about herself, she felt better inside and became much more confidant.

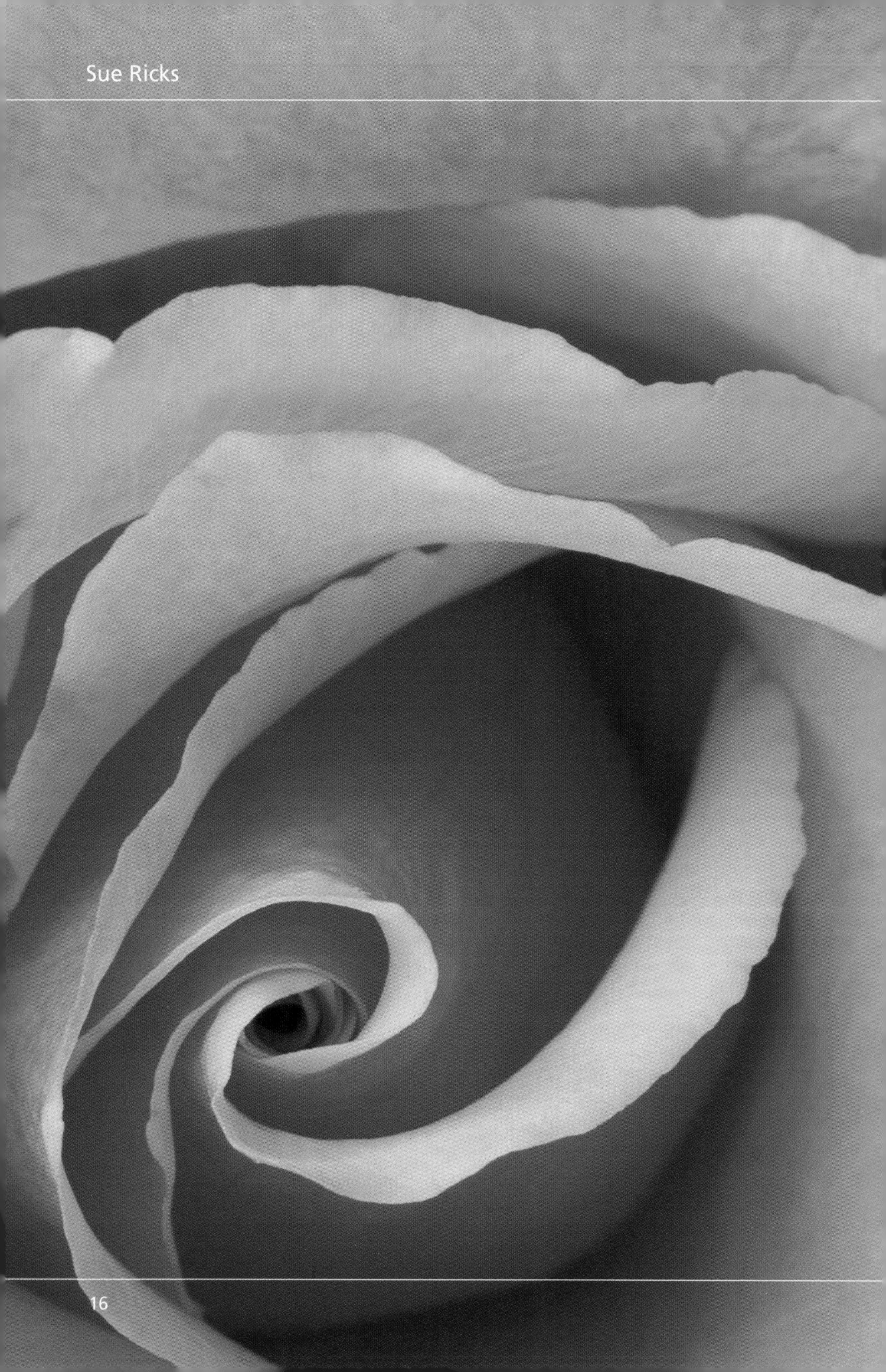

Now that you have one thing you like about you, it is time to add another!

Think about one more thing you like about you.

2) _____

Some more examples:

> I love my smile, my nails, my strong arms.
> I love my ability to mend things, use computers, write letters.
> I love my ability to dance, appreciate beauty, make things.
> I love my creativity, persistence, eye for detail.
> I love my ability to listen, be there for my friends.
> I love my care for my pet, my home, my health.
> I love my ability to play the piano, fish, play golf.

It is important that you disregard any negative comment or belief that anyone else has given you or that you have given yourself. For example, someone may have told you that you have horrible hair but you believe you have nice hair. 'I like my hair' could be one of the things you like about yourself because it is always what you believe that matters, not anyone else.

Any statement ending in "but ...." can be abbreviated to finish at the end of the positive statement i.e. "I like my smile but I don't smile enough" can be abbreviated very successfully to a simple "I like my smile". Alternatively you could leave that altogether and choose another more helpful and fulfilling statement, i.e. "I like my sense of humour". So remember that if something comes into your mind that is followed by a "but" i.e. "I like my ability to laugh but have nothing to laugh about" then I suggest you delete it and choose an alternative. It may be better to focus on something entirely different, i.e. "I always remember my family's birthdays."

I promise that it becomes easier with practice! When you can say two things you like about you, it is easier to find more things you like about you.

List the two things you like/love about you.
(Repetition is a perfect way of allowing this habit to become real)

1)_____

2)_____

Nearly there!

The final part of this stage is to think about a third thing that you like about you.

Again this could be a part of your personality, appearance, something you can do, a talent or something else.

3)_____

So now you are totally safe as you can choose to think about three things that you like about your life and three things that you like about you.

Practice saying these three things that you like about your life and yourself:

1)

2)   } I like about my life

3)

. . . .

1)

2)   } I like about me

3)

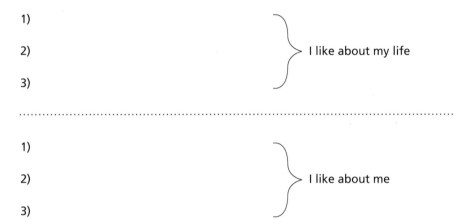

These are your 'life savers' and you can think about them whenever you need to boost yourself.

Any time that you notice that you are focusing on something negative, you can choose to alter your attention and distract yourself with something more pleasant and helpful to think about. This will raise your energy and give you greater clarity of thought.

You will be more likely to make good decisions if you are feeling more positive and better about yourself and your life.

You now have three 'externals', i.e. things you like about what is around you. The reason they are 'external' is because they are separate from yourself and they live around you. For example, your family, friends or pets etc, have to exist in order for you to love them and although they are part of your life, they are separate from your own existence. However, your sense of humour or ability to cook, fix computers etc, does not rely on anyone or anything else to be true. These are 'internal' qualities, dependent only upon you.

We all know that if a child has tumbled then we will usually comfort them, attempt to take their pain away and then distract the child so that they do not think about the hurt anymore. We can treat ourselves in a similar way.

If you are thinking about something that is not pleasant then you can distract yourself by thinking of your 'life savers'. When you think about these subjects you keep yourself in a better state of mind to cope with all the events and experiences of life. You will also be in a better state of mind to make a sensible decision.

The aim of this simple program is not to pretend that life is always okay (because it is not). Life is often challenging, however, this program gives you the simple steps and 'tools' or props to help you cope with your life at any given moment. They help you to acknowledge what is bad and then assist you to get into the right frame of mind to refocus on your strengths, give yourself an energy boost, distract yourself and help you to move forward in a better way.

It is a good idea to thoroughly learn the three things that you like about you and your life because sometimes the unexpected happens and you can quickly retrieve your 'life savers'. Learning these will be invaluable and will make the process of remembering your life savers much more effective.

When you are asked a question such as, "what is 3x3?" – you will probably respond immediately with "9". This is because you have learnt the times table at school and the answer just popped up. However, if you are asked, "what is 3+3+1?" - you would have to work it out and it may take a second or two longer to come up with the answer of 7.

This is similar to your 'life savers' because the better they have been committed to memory, the faster you can retrieve them. This means that when life happens (i.e. you need help to keep your energy up or improve your mood) you can easily remember your lifesavers, rather than having to delve into the filing cabinet of your mind to search for what they were.

If you are feeling down, it can be hard to think of anything at all that you like about your life or yourself! This is exactly why it is brilliant when you have learnt your 'life savers' and they pop up instantly and get you to a better place emotionally and mentally.

The quicker you recall, the quicker you develop your resources to cope with any situation in a better frame of mind. You will be more grounded and able to focus more accurately, thereby enhancing your decision-making abilities. Thinking about good aspects will enrich the possibilities of your actions and thoughts.

This technique will:

> Raise your self-esteem and immediately make you feel better about yourself. When you feel good about yourself, everything in life improves.
> You attract more positive energy, people and experiences into your life.
> You welcome new challenges and ways of making your life even better.
> Your relationships improve and you are able to communicate more effectively with everyone around you.

Working on this new level will in turn lead to more confidence in you and in the world. You will feel protected and reassured that, even if everything seems to be going terribly wrong, you still have three things you really like about your life and indeed, three things you really like about yourself. You are safe!

Richard was having a hard time at work and struggled to think about anything that was remotely acceptable in his working environment. We went through the three-step process and he realised that he had lots going for him. He soon noticed that he has been focusing on what was wrong and what he was worried about, rather than what was okay. He was previously 'feeding' the things he disliked about work and therefore making more of them. During our discussions he came up with the following 'life savers':

I love my motorbike, I love my guitar and I love my digital camera.

and

I love my beard, I love my ability to process information and I love my sense of humour.

Simply by repeating these thoughts in his head, he had created a whole new approach for himself at work. He found he loved his work and was then given his ideal project!

Suggestions

You can learn your 'life savers' and always use the same ones or you can alter them regularly. Some people alter them daily and decide upon waking what their 'life savers' will be for the day.

You will find that once you start doing this it will get easier and easier for you to come up with more things that you like about yourself. You will notice more things that you like about your life and it will be easier for you to list your many blessings.

> Practice saying these out loud and repeating them mentally.
> Stand in front of the mirror and repeat them or do this with a friend.
> Tell each other what you like about your lives and what you like about yourself.
> You may feel uncomfortable about doing this initially but you will find that as you both do this you give each other permission to like yourselves and this in turn helps you to be proud of these things.
> It can really help to reaffirm the good in your life and in yourself by sharing it with a friend or partner.

A word of caution – only do this with someone who genuinely wants to improve his or her life too – not everyone is ready to take that responsibility.

Step Three

When you have learnt and remembered your safe things to think about, you can distract yourself or dwell on something that will keep your energy up and help you to think clearly about whatever you need to deal with now. Your energy is now 'higher' and you are more able to think clearly about whatever you need to do. In order to be able to do this you need to be focused and thinking about the present moment.

Where am I now?

Ask yourself, "Where am I now?" NOTE: - If you ask your brain a question, it will always answer. However, your brain can delete a statement. You may say "I'm sitting in the lounge" and your brain will not register any reply as none is needed, but with a question your brain will search for and provide an answer.

When you ask yourself "where am I now?" you will use your senses to check where you are. Physically noticing where you are may stop you from worrying about the past/future.

People are often mentally living in either the past or the future. A great way of getting into the present moment is to ask yourself, "where am I now?" and think, for example, "I am sitting down on this chair in a room, reading this book". Or you may be driving and be aware that you are sitting on the seat in the car with your hands on the steering wheel.

Notice your surroundings right now. What can you see, hear, smell and feel etc? When you check what your senses can tell you, this means that you are in the 'now'. 'Now' is the only time that you can make a difference to your future. You cannot change the past and the future has not happened yet. However, you are 'now' making a difference to what you are creating and attracting in your future.

Whatever approach you decide to try, if you ask the question and use your senses, it is sure to be effective.

Avoiding Issues

One of my clients once asked me if this means that you just live life with 'rose coloured spectacles' and therefore never see anything bad in life by always purely seeing the good.

I think this is a fair question, however it is important that we acknowledge the bad (or inappropriate) things and issues that are in our lives. We need to be aware of what these are and do whatever is necessary to assist mankind and ourselves in dealing with them. However, once we have acknowledged the negative and taken the appropriate action, we can then choose to think good and positive thoughts. This allows the focus of our attention to be on healthier mental patterns that actually grow, support and empower us to make better decisions.

Marion worried that she would miss things that may cause her a problem if she did not keep watch for things that may hurt or trouble her. She had spent her life worrying and often had loads to worry about, however, during our session she began to see that she was attracting 'doom and gloom' because that was all she thought about. It was very hard for her to dare to think about some good things but immediately she had a great result as she thought about nature and dance. Within a week of changing her thinking she has been asked to help a friend with a workshop and made new friends, earned some extra money and found she was really good at organizing!

Making Decisions

In some cases, we dwell so much on the problem that we can actually start to become overwhelmed by it. It may become virtually impossible to think clearly and creatively about what to do next. It is therefore helpful to acknowledge the problem and then lift your energy and your ability to look after yourself by thinking about your 'life savers'. You can return to thinking about your problem again but by this time you will have a much greater clarity and focus.

It is difficult to think about how to resolve an issue when you have negative thoughts rolling around in your head. A much better way to sort the problem is to 'pump' yourself up by thinking about good thoughts and then see how much easier it is to move forward and make a healthy decision. Remember if you dwell on your problem you are actually going to feed it and therefore make it worse.

Acknowledging Problems

Do what you can in a short period of time to resolve or affect your issue. If you cannot resolve it quickly, then switch off the emphasis and avoid putting more energy and effort into it. A healthier alternative is to switch off your negative thoughts by re-focusing your mind and energy and then proceed to the next step.

Pay close attention to where you are and what you are doing, also notice what you are actually thinking about. Many people's problems are drawn from the past and are projected into the future. The key to making a difference is to be 'positively' in the present.

Projected worries can be crippling to people so it is much better to focus on what is okay and search for positives.

Chapter Three – Helpful Hints

The following table shows helpful exercises for you to study once you have your 'three lifesavers'. It will be beneficial for you to look at these frequently, especially at the start of reading this book.

In time, you may learn these questions by heart and no longer need to refer to the book. An ideal goal is to know these lifesavers so well that they are recalled immediately at any time. Practise doing the questions and become an expert.

The exercises will help you to:

> Keep a check on what you are thinking
> Notice where your energy is going
> Realise what you are attracting into your life

They also help you to identify the areas which you need to improve, such as daily negative thoughts so that subsequent days get better and better. Become an expert in the making!

These exercises will also enhance your awareness of your thought processes and bring you personal power.

Awareness of your thoughts and actions brings personal power that will give you the ability to change, enjoy and maximise your life and all your options.

Sue Ricks

More Helpful Hints

Ask yourself	Experience	Solution
What have I focused on today?	Energy follows thought, so what are you feeling?	Focus on the positive things and thoughts.
What am I paying attention to now?	Is this healthy for me to be thinking about?	Think about good things, (look around you) and recall your three choices.
What percentage of today have I been thinking (and directing my thoughts) positively?	Aim to increase the percentage of positive thought. Positive attracts positive.	Do a personal audit of energy allocation! See the increase over time.
What good can I see in 'X'?	'Find' the good in any individual/ situation – everyone benefits.	i.e. "X..... has lovely eyes."
What am I looking at daily?	Can I improve it? (Make it more attractive, organised etc.) Your environment affects your energy.	Look around you to find helpful things to notice, i.e. a plant, picture, an ornament.
How long will I allow myself to think about this 'issue/problem?'	Allow yourself an allocated number of minutes to be miserable, angry, worried etc, and then make a decision to focus on anything good.	Consciously alter your train of thought, in order to get into a good state of mind.
Would a support 'buddy' help me?	Identify someone who is generally positive and cheerful to be a support 'buddy' to help you stay positive if the going gets tough.	Ask them to listen and then after an agreed length of time, help you to change the subject and this will help you change your thought patterns.

Support Buddies are invaluable. Remember that a fireman throws you a lifeline – he doesn't get into the 'bog' with you!

Three Simple Steps: Big Difference

The simplicity of the three steps program to happiness is delightful.

All you need to do is:

1. Acknowledge the negative thoughts/actions
2. Take appropriate action
3. Use your 'life saver' positive plan.

"Life saver" Plan

1. What do I like about my life? (x3)
2. What do I like about me? (x3)
3. Where am I now?

When you learn your life saver plan and remember to alter your focus to positive thoughts, you will find that you are more focused, with greater stability in life and, of course, you will be so much more content.

Have fun experimenting and see your life improve!

Be Happy.

My hope is that this will be a constant reminder for you. Maybe you will read this book and then some time later come across it again and remember to use the suggestions.

The book can act as a memory jogger for all of us.

For more information on Sue's work please see her website
www.suericks.com

For information on Gentle Touch™ Reflexology see
www.suericks.com and www.g-t-r.org

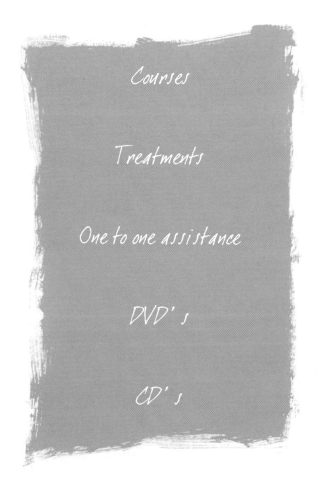

Courses

Treatments

One to one assistance

DVD's

CD's